"Aristotle claimed in the Poetics that learning gives the human animal the liveliest pleasure. *Breakfast in Fur* celebrates this strange gift. The pleasures of this book surprise and delight as they defy the conventions of self-searching and introspection. Jessica Murray plumbs discordant sources in our strange world, from pornography to ceramic art, from marriage to childbirth to friendship to fleeting glance. This is a spiritual autobiography of great daring that celebrates the well-made mistake rather than protecting the untaken chance. At its best moments, it is coldly wild, and full of vivid experiment."

—Katie Peterson, author of *Life in a Field*

"*Breakfast in Fur* offers its readers not just a view into life deeply examined but also life deeply imagined. These powerful poems masterfully make the strange familiar and the familiar strange, raising epistemological and ethical questions as they often hover in that hour before birdsong when the borders between dream and reality and life and art seem to waver. Murray reminds us that to be fully awake and human is to travel to the interior only to find there is no interior. Always an elsewhere, further off, deeper in. We will never look at the firefly or the wasp or ourselves the same way again."

—Kathleen Graber, author of *The Eternal City*

Breakfast in Fur

Breakfast in Fur
by Jessica Murray
Copyright © Jessica Murray 2022

ISBN 978-0-913123-25-6

First published by Galileo Books in 2022
freegalileo.com
murrayjessica.com

Cover image: Ravine Park, 2020, by Valerie Fowler. Ink, watercolor,
and colored pencil on cotton rag paper.
Book design by Adam Robinson & Melissa Thornton

A portion of book sales goes to Urban Roots

Breakfast in Fur

JESSICA MURRAY

for Eric and Des

Table of Contents

...the wind finds something to ping
or the pinging thing finds the wind

we're all looking for a body
or a means to make one sing

—Bill Callahan, *The Sing*

THE FOURTH GEORGIC

Sometimes a dolphin in captivity will take
one last look around, close her eyes, and sink
to the bottom of the tank.

At the beach, we just wanted to know
why the seaweed was heaping itself
onto the shore in thick slick silks.

When we started out, to protect myself
I said, marriage is a set of limitations.
Something about all the wires

cutting into the visual realm
suggested new forms:
clouds rose dense and vertical,

the horizon drew breath,
had mass—aren't we two small bodies in wild space,
one organ in love with the earth?

We sat in the sun, felt its steady stroke
sweetness beneath our skin.
Soon, we would go inside, kiss each

other's eyes. But first I wanted
to read you
the story of the bees, which doubles.

A collateral of bulls. The story is told twice, once
as a series of imperatives and again
so that the real ending is always beginning:

Everywhere in the bellies of the victims
Bees buzzing in the fermenting viscera
And bursting forth from the ruptured sides in swarms

That drift along like enormous clouds in the sky
And come together high in the top of a tree
And hang in clusters from the swaying branches.

There were no trees on that island
but the salt spray burned white,
an image in negative against the sky.

We looked out from the porch, tenting the vantage
point with our hands as the wind rushed in
on invisible pinions.

The water, if we were willing to swim out far enough,
seemed clear. But the wind made talking unpredictable:
We didn't know what we were hearing.

AVATAR

Because I want to know what it's like
these days, I ask my husband to watch
        some porn with me, recs from
the sex-positive shop. Has it gotten kinder,
        more complicated by ambition?
When I look back at that woman
        in my 20s, I try to look kindly,

        with qualified affection. I was lucky
to watch porn with good men. Meaning, I guess,
        I chose them. Thinking back, the sound quality
conjures a cassette tape that's been erased
        and re-recorded on, brittle as candy.
Plot that savaged credulity. An aesthetic perspective
        that panted and squeaked

        between too much and not enough
irony. Something contemptuous
        multiplied like spoors in all that water
and oxygen, as though the producer were the kind
        of person who would show you
around his house, saying, *look how much I paid
        for all this shit.*

        Eric says sure, asks me if I remember
the VHS tape I lugged around for years.
        Stuffed in the back of a drawer, wrapped
in a moth-ravaged sweater wedged in a closet.
        I bloomed with mild anxiety every time
family visited, every time we scraped
        suitcases down the steps,

as if someone might break
into our house steal all our stuff, and leave
the tape in silent exoneration
for the authorities to find. The more it gave
itself away, the less I knew
how to palm it off. I could find a copy again, circle it
from the viewpoint of a red-tailed hawk,

but one who's not really hungry,
or stoop, a harrier hanging on
the underground's breath and scurry.
I can't say with any certainty I know
what I'm doing. Is the way
one if by eye, two if by ear?
When I recall the tape, I see a woman

in a dress the color of a heated pool.
She's paused awkwardly if
dramatically on a sweeping stair.
Somewhere offstage a clock strikes.
The man is in costume, too, resembling formal wear.
Called *Dawn of a New Century,* the locomotive
puffed into view.

BOX MAY CONTAIN A BABY GOAT, A BOOK LOVER, A NAGGING SUSPICION, AN ACT, MAYBE FORMALDEHYDE

A baby goat, *whoops*, falling off the side of a mountain.
A possum that looks like it's sleeping
         on the underside of a speedbump
as the moon draws its curtain.
         A quorum of strangers pooling money, can-do,
and Labrador-retriever-level enthusiasm
         because love, or something like it, bade them.

A book-lover entering the wrong library,
beck of the wrong librarian. No borrowing,
         only pages awry she can
never return. An image of a child so bereft
         that to look, not to look, is another violation.
The word *found* scrawled in grateful,
         disbelieving red across a taped-up sign.

A nagging suspicion that the donation has disappeared
into the bureaucratic mechanisms,
         was too inconsequential, no matter,
to provide one half-cracked egg of relief.
         A hope that the Flock of Chicks, the share
of a Milk Menagerie is a reprieve for someone
         who won't grow to despise the premise of you.

An act so flensed with self-loathing and despair
you will feel a physical sadness
         when it presses into your thoughts.
Bravery that shatters you in your kitchen,
         where sometimes you *bake a cake or something*.
A video of a rescued dog whose final breaths
         are framed to culminate in the honest ask.

A malingering scent, maybe formaldehyde,
that ruins the effect of the hastily painted little cakes and ales.
Diagrams that at first glance seem to show
the complete assembly, but whose perspective
is all wrong. A kitchen sash flung open, through which
sunlight and crows are falling. A belief, impossible
to prove, at least one piece is missing.

NOISOME PESTILENCE

Through slats in the blinds I looked up
to see hornets building their nest
between two rickety panes of glass.

—Irrational? I wanted
it done.

When the hornets were alive,
I took their presence like a slight.
Unapologetically personal.

Dead, they brought no relief.

This made sense, for now I had
the feeling something was taking me personally.
As though I were responsible
for the way they clung to their
doomed little cells.

How needless it seems to me now,
needless but unavoidable,
how they hang suspended,
swaddled in sunlight and esters.

A RAGGED TIME

My husband knows one line to one hymn,
Thy sea is great, our boats are small,
Thy sea is great, our boats are small.
He sings it nightly until the baby sleeps.
The room is dimly lit by the pulse
of an artificial seascape: turtle, jellyfish, clamshell.
From the other room, I hear his voice.
Tender, softly accosting,
little green crest capped with foam.

The song cannot reconcile lifejackets
in the picture windows of Turkey,
a boy washed up faced down in the sand.
Whose body, now, makes an elastic breath that swims
beyond the just-the-facts-ma'am clangor,
as though we could
get to the bottom of something
too deep to sound.
While *je suis Parisienne* was trending,
I was walking through a field of wildflowers.
Dragonflies bent the falling light,
a body of water moved, grooves in a record.

Lazy-eyed, accusingly shaped, dotted
with an enlarged heart—
the compassion machine, like any god,
is a kind of wish fulfillment:
each time the world splinters, the machine
reproduces by division.

Profligate as cedar pollen, as ragweed
in a ragged time,
it disperses molecules on which
synthetic parasites enter the bloodstream.

The machine is earnest on the subject of origins:
reduce yourself to an object
means you love the world.

Shoes tucked behind a scrim of viscera,
Doris Salcedo's *Atrabiliarios*.
Hapless shirts coated in plaster,
stacked on rebar.
Dark wood worn with the disappeared's touch,
Untitled.   *Untitled.*

The machine sniffs. *Emotional truth
is the poor man's fact.*

I object, I refuse.

Inside my body, the muscle-memory
of contraries, of pleasures
struggles not to be consumed by parasitic eggs
mouthing my flesh toward use.

Each mouth has its say:
I'm here to help, friend.
You can have the ocean—fat, slapping seaweed,
a crashing brackish green—
any implacable ache!
For it, you must wear this 20th century haircloth:

how else will we know
that you know
that we know
you're guilty?

My body hums a larval hunger.

I've tried, I say, eyeing the haircloth.
Thinking I'm holding it at arm's length,
only to see, from a craftily placed mirror,
myself gesturing pathetically.

Trees in a forest feed the cut stumps around them.
Humpback whales loll about with their penises
draped all over each other.

I would like to know
how old the oldest living jellyfish is,
how many lovers have trailed their hands across the bark
of the world's oldest tree.

What good does it do to remember
the suffering only at their point of extremity?
Don't make of them an unlikeness.
Don't waste the materials at hand.

When I dream my own dead,
they are not feather vane or golden hollow.
With inscrutable innards, they circle
uncanny landscapes. They play at air
beneath the living bird at play.

The machine is an error in any valuation of safety.
All we can offer is a contingent protection,
sometimes after the fact.

Like Salcedo's, Kathy Butterly's forms are another kind of fact
the dead also consecrate.

Peach and aquamarine glazes, those *verges
of seas*, delirious surfaces.

Her matter, *bulges, protrusions, bodily fluids*,
a play on joy, *joue*.

The machine plays me for a fool.
Object, refuse.

Be daring as Hannah Wilke,
I tell myself, composing her naked figure
at Cadaqués, echo and jesting clarion.
Love, let's watch again (it wasn't just a dream)
midnight's leatherback hatchlings
drag themselves toward every lost mother.

I listen to the way my husband's song repeats
and in repeating a familiar
changing, closing the baby's eyes
into darkness, night, solitude.
Each of us makes what we can

with what we have—the song retrieved,
perhaps, from a place of incoherence, or worse.
Also, second chances, wrong turns,
the long way around.

Let me sing, too, against the stillness
of any dream for a child's safety.
Safety, my love, is a myth. The jellyfish
perishes. Always, something wants in,
out—the body inside the body like a shell.
Softness exposed is to live in the world.
Love begins as a single note.

UNDERSTUDY

All morning, I have been trying
to untether the bird from its perch.

BORROWED FEATHERS

I have a friend who's in the middle of self-invention: early marriage, older man, fifteen years, children. Take risks, we say. Be vulnerable. But there's an energy here, a *tsk-tsk* in the erasable marker's squeaking tip. The copier runs and runs its sneering wit.

Boredom, curiosity, avarice: so many cats mother invention. I'm thinking of my friend, myself, people I read about in books. Jean-Marie Jacquard, who lost his money, took up arms, watched his child die beside him.

In the aftermath, his machine: hole or no hole, hole or no hole for thousands of cardboard cards wound round a spindle. An emptiness into which a prong could enter or be denied. The telos of ones and zeros takes grief as its genesis. Look at that image woven into the silk, that slippery sheen. It wants to be touched, a shaken hound. It wants to be etched, stone.

In *How Forests Think*, I kept reading to understand how forests think. Looking for a little self-help. But forests don't think qua forests, silly! Rather everything in them thinks. The unfamiliar is all around us. My friend has an expensive body, looks good in stilettos.

Her boasts? The wrong brags for the new crowd.

Although the tedium was not so corrosive it prevented drawboys from keeping nests of sparrows, days at the loom before Jacquard's invention were measured in inches.

Quickly, little sparrows, careful, now.

An error in the warp thread raised or lowered, to mar the image, impossible to detect in *medias res*. Or only in *medias res*. The mistake revealed itself, as it so often does only once. The weave was finished.

TOOTHPICK, LEMON JUICE

—for Caroline Herschel

No one goes to the opera anymore.
But I would have liked to hear
your soprano in its century
among the fashionable,
seen you tressed, black silk dress,
onstage at Bath.

I've read your diaries, notebooks,
ledgers, letters.
Even the gaps in the record.
We speculate, it's in our nature.

Just yesterday, the baby slept
in some other noon.
Rain puddled, bolts of raw black milk
unwindowed:

I peeled an orange in the stillness.
Come night, ticked a fine machinery.
So you never invented anything.
So you focused in a single vanishing point
your mother's cruelties
all the necessity
of the survivor's love.

You might be forgiven for having thought
you'd more or less married your brother.
Platonically.
For the sake of the unknown
entered and entering.

She would have you, darling,
unlettered, un-numbered,
to gasp for breath
the animal fat and ashes.

She gasped for breath
the animal fat and ashes.

Loneliness: one thing to push against.
You trained your eyes
deep in pockets
of fractious gasses.
Your art: to warp
if not transcend your family's careless edict.
A brutal usefulness.

Your brother paid your freedom, true—
released from one debt
into a more expansive one.

Your voice, they say, hastily trained
in stolen moments,
sounded green if beautiful
enough. But the abdomen, that seed
of mystery, of blood,
overruled the head:
sometimes we cannot leave for leaving.

Caroline, I wasn't sure how else to do this—

[   ]

THE RANK OF THINGS INDIFFERENT

I worked as a waitress in a coastal town. We groaned when a tour bus pulled up. Leaf-peepers ruined our shifts with their exacting arithmetic, their glosses on server-served rules of conduct. Yet they could surprise us with an offhand kindness, the depths of their appetites.

In Texas, a spike in juniper pollen has gifted me a soft-tissue injury from sneezing. Back home, the leaf season depends on complex weather systems. Did summer storms nourish the earth, the roots with rain enough? Or did a critical mass of tent moths thrive, defoliating first the wild black cherry, the hawthorn, then anything left with shade?

The wasps that prey on the larvae used to repulse me. It all repulsed me. The soft gray pouches—wombs crawling with half-formed matter—the wasps' neurological poisons, mummification or consumption of larvae alive from within. Although I know the wasps are just part of nature, it was hard to shake the sense there was something sinister about them.

The only way to guarantee a good tip from the tourists was to find yourself set up with a table of six or more, where an automatic gratuity could be included. Management did that for their friends, lifers like Susan or Sharon, whose hands were always shaking. I was too young for the coke of the 80s, when regulars might leave an 8-ball in a bathroom stall for a tip. Sharon died young from cancer. Kay, dramatic, acerbic, was always talking about her boyfriend to a small huddle of women, from which new girls like myself were excluded. How in the middle of their marathon sex, she would defecate on her boyfriend's face, a thin film of cellophane between them.

My husband and I have lived in seven states and three countries, which doesn't seem like very many. My sister's husband says we need to settle down, focus—stop pretending we have world enough and time to keep making choices. I thought about staying right there in that first town, not because I liked those women, though I did. How their choices—often impetuous, unlucky, irresponsible, naïve—made manifest their options. I didn't need to *sallie forth and see my adversaries.*

I changed my mind about the wasps when I learned the trees "call" them, alchemists of a delectable perfume when their limbs are under attack. Turns out, the wasps are practically gallant. Not only that, but the wasps themselves suffer from hyper-parasitism, where the colonizing wasp becomes a further wasp's victim. When I relay this to my husband, he says, *just when you think you know what side you're on, something changes.*

Shifts ended, we left through the back door. Cash that didn't have to be reported, the lie of free money. We sat breathing in the silence of our passenger seats. I am certain Kay would have never walked up to a table and given her name, unsolicited. She would have quit, cigarette already to her lips, before uttering, *I'll be taking care of you tonight.* The distance was more honest. In the packed-dirt parking lot, the moon had us clear in her sights. Beyond that, the terrible stars.

GOING FOR A SONG

We purchased the less sexual
feeder, without that suggestive,
bouncy sheath. We got the regular one
so when the lady squirrels
make their ever-rounder acrobatic leaps,
they can cling to their hard-won
sway, stuff their cheeks.
Birds watch, cheap trick.

·

A cheap shot is like a pun, the ear
scrambling the brain, like grain
alcohol, like jet lag. The blow
awkward never squared always
insists on following
drumroll and cymbal crash.
The way a late dove feels
the air before the red-shouldered hawk
and knows the band's all there.

·

You old cheap skate!
Don't you even want to know
what's on the menu?

THE STATE WITH THE PRETTIEST NAME:
A MANIFESTO

I went to Florida for a reunion with my friend
who was reuniting with *her* friend,
whose installation art I had admired—
the sculptor was more than an acquaintance, not a close friend.

I'd forgotten the rule about being friends with somebody else's friend.
The one where you imagine hanging out in equilateral,
only to discover everything's acute.
The sculptor found me tiresome, undisciplined.
I ruined the seriousness
that was supposed to be the principle fun.

Things were shaky as the three of us walked the beach
looking for dead fish, washed up detritus
and taking about our dreams.
Then ominous, then openly opposed between us—
our likes and dislikes, mine and the sculptor's,
couldn't be more different,

and, hence, took on moral dimensions.
Especially on the merits of Florida, the place
she was stranded.
Without her partner, removed from all urban culture.
Hand-painted signs, death to the unrepentant,
staked into the grass by no one you ever saw, where
nobody ever was.
The mirror for stimulation, loneliness.
How I loved it, I said, thinking of my husband,
the crushed perfume of the trees
dripping their resins and flush with insect life.
Vultures circling as if they were twirling invisible strands of hair,
cloudbanks that said, *go ahead, love,*
drink up, peel me back, no, drink your fill.

My problem according to the sculptor
was not with my personhood,
which after our confrontation she was at pains
to establish was especially Generous and Thoughtful
but for trying to talk about art
(around a campfire, even), with her and her students
when I had never been coached up.

In a way, she was right—but, then, it's a conundrum
because sometimes I want to talk about art, a difficult idea,
something I read,
even though I feel my coherence at suboptimal—
but not, like, gross—
conditions. Naturally, I suppose, this bothers people.
I think it's because I've done nothing
that would suggest anyone take me seriously.
I came late to the party, no one wants to sit around
and wait for me to get drunk.

Nonetheless, I am compelled to affirm
something in Kathy Butterly's work obligated me
to risk sounding the fool, to say,
I like this. I think you might like it, too.

There's something romantic about half-lives,
vulgar about doubling times.
I carried Butterly's work with me, *inside* of me,
to Florida, from Boston, where I first saw it,
then back to Boston for half a decade, from Boston
to Texas, where I live.
I live here, now.

AFTER READING SALLY MANN'S MEMOIR

The old story: pup taken in
by the dog-loving family and taught to kill
        by the pack's alpha female.
Unable to discern what's wild and therefore
        expendable, coaxed into a shallow pit
by the neighbor and shot, as is the rule.
        Other solutions take trial. Error. Faith. Money.

        Dear, you know me—another botched attempt
at the beautiful. All I've been thinking:
        how often we punish others
for what we can't express we find
        dangerous about their behavior.
Mann says photography is mechanized forgetting.
        What's fluid in time

        reduced to a point, obliterated.
Sometimes, I may seem to forget your kindness, attention.
        I have few photographs of them.
Is the risk the image of the dog
        sleeping sweetly under the table
may become more real but less familiar?
        Or is it vice versa,

        while the memory of the dog, aware
but not comprehending, his body falling
        almost preceding the silence that
fells it, can be replayed to what use to no end?
        Love, pictured, unpictured
plays tricks on imagination. After the photographs
        of Mann's children became famous,
people thought they knew them.

I'LL BE

Hard winters I've slid
my delicious foot
inside the snuggest
fur-lined mouth.
Despite the seasonal cliff-
notes of crosses and stars,
the sky is less brass section
than oracle.
Blind, bullish clouds
obscure the trick
of the opening,
the way it plays at

serving you.

HOUR BEFORE BIRDSONG

I

The baby, sick, and you ironing your clothes
while the dogs make eyes.
I'm running the shower, I'm leaving
a message, exhausted, leaving
with the baby, with you, start over, new life.
In the evening, I remember the half-loaf of rye
from the bakery. It's toasting, now,
a creamy, salt-flecked butter softened
all day on the counter. And who has opened
the blinds unthinking, opened
the blinds to the street,

a little darkness,   no birdsong,
          a little light slipping in.

The tenants before us shellacked
black film over the narrow back window.
We can look out, no one sees in.
The cardinal with his dripping oars
rows into the yellow jasmine and out again.
The baby and I are tracing our trapezoid
through the rooms. I am trying to connect
the point where the shape starts
to the precise point it ends.

May we fall   through
        oblivion.

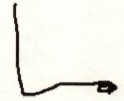

III

Alone, I speak to every vital thing:
hello, squirrel,   *hello, crow.*
Go away, beetle.
Hello, hello to pairs of cardinals, *hello, hello.*
Sometimes in the afternoon an episode of *True Blood*,
a little bored with itself and not paying
too much attention, ends with a wooden stake,
a gash of sticky viscera.
Nobody wants to die, not even the detective.
Like a Nauman neon sign, the shorthand blinks

sex   remember   freedom
    enter   danger   pleasure

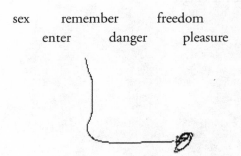

FOUR-AND-TWENTY

A book on your chest, you've fallen asleep
as you do every night. Pages deckled
as pie crust.

I turn off your light, close the book.
Then, as now, the things you like are varied,
simple, generous, open.

Open your body for me, miraculous blackbird.
Red winged, unbowed eye,
sing your dainties before the king.

Dear —

You're gone, and I'm chasing sensation—
Lowell's rat, still on the trip. In one book, a
man travels from his university in Quebec City to
Ecuador to study a people on the threshold
of disappearing into the contemporary. A myth
he recounts quickens the rhetoric: two unequal
forces in the landscape — a people, a group of
demons — come face to face. The people, "ringed
the tree with big piles of hot peppers, which they set on
fire to choke out the demons. All the demons plummeted
to earth except one. When the last juri-juri fell to
the ground, she assumed the shape of a beautiful
white woman. A young man took pity on her."

You can imagine what happens next. Marriage,
children. Then the demon eats the children by the
river where they bathe. In fact, she sucks out
their brains. Next, her husband's. That's how
I'll die, I keep thinking, his little seated
behind me, fanning out my objecthood. Do I
lack affect? my smooth, like his, won't stop
it's compulsive yawning. He didn't say
why are you eating me? only "you are eating me."
How can I even be sure I'm not automata,
it's me that pens this? your madame
Tussaud

Dear —

It was useless as shouting at a horror
movie, watching the man extending his
hand accelerating the hand's own demise.
Of course, I understood. Pressing his body
against a devouring dark and calling it
charity. His face in my half-turned mirror,
that hopeful, glancing light, made him my
familiar. Slippery myth reinvents its
meaning — as soon as it's issued, warning
begets invitation.

I hear voices, anxiety dream of impossible
chorus. Exercise and clean living. Centuries of it,
sniffing whiskey rings dried in tinkling porcelain.
When I'm sleepy, I find it hard to sleep: my
ears pick up the half-heard plea, I'm "bu-rning
hot." The story's protagonist enters the ashes
of burned peppers with an urge to protect
what would destroy him. The word I was
looking for is confluence.

your nightengale

Dear —

I cannot wait you anymore, kissing
Yu Xuanji through luscious tears and
sending love letters to the rain. I traveled
to the interior only to find there is no
interior. You knew it all along, pocketing
your silence. Here, in the night's gaseous
flame, our son puts his hands in my
hair — mama's hair, mama's hair — fingers
on my skull tiny spoons against a soft boiled
egg. Careful, little one. The man from the
city, the man from the forest. I saw them
here. Superimposed, like the book's fabled
were — puma, doubled blindness in the
night's flashing.

Not spoons, but an earthmover scooping up
great chunks of dirt. How gently the prongs
of the bucket — untangling fingers, teeth in
a certain face, did their work. I felt giddy,
a summer's vertigo. The earth forcing its
way into that trembling mouth. The earth
dug up, dug up, turned over. Make me new.

SIGN ON THE DOOR

In the neighbor's pecan tree one dove
fat as a powdered donut
hops on the back of another.
They can't be having sex, I think, it looks too silly,
the this-must-get-to-that
too precarious. Him flapping, teetering,
trying to balance on a glass marble,
him trying to be the marble.

But the way the male's head bobs
begins to remind me of a certain missionary style.
This morning's proselytizer,
trying to peek his head in as he's headed up the walk.
Rapping on the window, unsure
whether he saw something or imagined it—
movement, light, behind the stiff-backed curtains.

SKINNY DIPPING

I ask my husband if he remembers an article
about scientists filming some whales
      at rest, penises draped all over each other.
He says he doesn't think so,
      not looking up from the cutting board
where he's chopping fruit.

I tell him it sounded interesting,
that I keep imagining him and some friends
      floating in the ocean
with 10-foot-long penises. Finally, a smile.
      How, exactly, would that work? he asks me.
I wave my hand in that gesture half-dismissive,

      half magnanimous. Besides, I tell him,
it's not sexual, just the sex organ
      being used non-procreatively
in high-spirited friendship. Enter my husband,
      his raised eyebrow.
Though part of the joke is I'm always looking

      for a little action in unexpected places,
I can't help feeling something kin
      to a birthright, a secular psalm.
How I wish for him to blink his eyes open
      to a furiously scoured sea, bright, blinding salt spray.
The faces of his friends who sustain

      and buoy him. That their skin might touch.
That their love be reflected and amplified
      in the drops of water
that fall from their lashes. That I might be
      the figure who watches only him.
The pineapple tumbles.

HIS NETHERLANDS

So much washes up on shore
he has opened museums,
contents little nests
to stand in for infinity:

heaps of seaworthy rope
in bright bowlines, half-hitches.
Driftwood and flotsam,
plastic brushes with which to scrub
all manner of surfaces.
Photographs, shoes, one rotary phone.
Slim delicate anchors,
buoys faded to the pastels of birthday candles.

He's happy to advise
how best to send messages:
pebble-bottomed vessels
so that the current,
not the wind, carries them.

Sometimes, a cargo ship
will spill a container of unasked for,
unimagined riches.
Sometimes, the water returns
the limp body of a swimmer.
Drop what you like into any current,
but don't toss out anything
about which you might have second thoughts.
He keeps what the sea gives,
some things the sea never gives back.

PARK WILLOWS, MAY 2017

If you want to keep me, you gotta, gotta, gotta, gotta,
got to love me harder

My two favorite strangers
arrive with their shy, sweet father.
His lowrider with bent dorsal fins,
his pack of cigarettes soft,
tucked in his slim shirt pocket.

His son and mine bluster across the playground,
sugared locusts. His daughter
throws or kicks harmless
things in my direction, almost-
accidentally runs up against
or into me.
I liked mothers, too, when I was a child,
the permission to trust
someone else's body
casually, like sunlight.

The father says, *when you're on*
the swings and going high,
it makes all the juices in your stomach swirl
together, makes you feel kind
of funny. All of us swing
in different time and direction,
sprung keys on a busted piano.

And when his son starts yelling,
snow! It's snowing! even though
it's just a few white
willow seeds brushing our cheeks,
I taste citrus so bittersweet
I am suddenly breathing
under snow drifts
pressing down their blue weight.

Bodies, now. Those little girls
on the cusp of something.
Blazed with music, movement,
with the giddiness of being
among others who shared
a night they were already enlarging
with a look, practicing,
practicing, the caught glance
of any beautiful stranger.

Mercy, now. Let mercy be
in the ashes, the smallest
ash that fell,
and the smallest ash that lifted.
Here in Arcadia,
there's nothing left
between the snow and roses.

CURTAIN CALL

Yellow sparks trail off in soft vocables,
right through the cocktail hour's wet blaze.
All that unpredictable light!
Courtship and disaster,
cold hard fact of illuminated things
the more unapproachable
the more we know.

To ward off the *phidippus audax*, the jumping spider,
photuris fireflies need lucibufagins, sour-
tasting steroids produced
by the *photinus*, their kissing cousins.
To get the steroids, the female *photuris* learned
to mimic the *photinus'* amorous signals—
to attract the male *photinus* then consume him.

Clever, terrifying. But there's a coda:
the watchful male *photuris* began to imitate
the male *photinus*, in order to attract
a hunting female *photuris* to mate with.
And the *photinus* males began to imitate
female *photuris* imitating male *photinus*
to scare other *photinus* males away…

Luciferase, luciferin. Substrate
and enzyme. Add adenosine
triphosphate, and the tiny bodies light up, the fathomless
night stage brought to the understory.
Each dusk, games of gender, intrigue, deception
expend themselves on gentle vectors,
thin slips of sun-soaked grass.

Who hasn't been devoured bending down
for the wrong kind of benediction?
        If one sits in the tiny blaze,
cool to the touch, night may shed
            its ordinary edges, but impossible to say
            whether the naked performance
is marked more by tragedy or romance.

        The only thing clear as the ice-cube
eddying in its velvety spirits
            is something banal about cruelty
and gratuitousness. The spider, if it weren't
            sleeping, could watch this
            with its eight all-seeing eyes. Jaws a dreamy
green, opalescent as a razor clam's shell.

HUNGER, AN ANNIVERSARY

I was as the songbird:

alight in the midstory, assessing angles,
nesting in the complex mess. Planets ticked,
continents shifted.

Earth awhile with two south poles. Havocked
tracking systems.
        The rain rained down and rearranged us.

We turned in tandem, sleep
a machine to repair the dreaming.

Wasn't I the bird's eye?
In that ambient light, I understood.
Distance, velocity, direction.

The rain, first harder, then softer,
seeped into the earth each channel, each cavity.

        You are to me the orange
fruit, scooped into the mouth

of a starving man, a free man.
Who knew my earth.
Who sowed the seeds, who sheltered them.

BREAKFAST IN FUR

I

A scat fetish. Its longevity—reaction videos,
imitations—what can you make of it,
a horizon, this contrail gone soft, butchering
indeterminate chunks of sky?

The way my composition students
whispered about it—
grainy footage, I thought,
of things that happen to girls and women.
Things we're told to mind
or find ourselves gotten into.

Cup both receptacle and vessel,
it's a thing divided, immobilized by two masters.
A professional production. Meaning,
there was consent. Some sort
of compensation. A handshake.

I spent years, ambivalent ones,
talking to the front row, asking those
focused gazes to consider how choice
is often heavily processed,
conditioned as the ingénue's hair
during Oscar night.

One pornographic actress-producer insists,
If a female porn performer is depicting
"passivity," she is playing a role because
it's her job to do so. If and when
she experiences acute discomfort
or exploitation on the job, that is a labor issue.
I want to know the pornographer's intentions.

II

Sometimes I've tried to join a group
by signaling my willingness
to be excluded from it. Where is the line
between an honest expression
of what can feel innate, elemental,
to be turned on by what is forbidden,
or by the hunger of another person's vulnerability,
and cruelty, abuse?

I misremembered an article about male orcas
pleasuring themselves and other orcas.
I'd wanted to romanticize it.
Turning the orcas into humpback whales,
de-escalating the nature of touch,
framing the whales as avatars
in an updated, watery Pantisocracy or Brook Farm.

Things I'm prone to imagining everybody desires—
friendly sex without consequences,
sex with the best kinds of consequences with someone you love,
community, ecology, economic freedom
without injury.

Whales only ever seem to be taking care of each other,
or even somebody else, some stranger.
Call it instinct, though vast furls of the ocean are no more
known to us than sun-washed quadrants on a map.
In the Pacific, orca echolocation whistles and clicks
in fellowship—resident pods
threatened by Bigg's killer whales.
They hunt the soundscape almost in silence,
preying on other mammals.

Bigg's whales used to be called transients,
as though they were runaways or orphans
whose behavior had been shaped by something unspeakable:
survival without love, tutelage,
green thoughts in a green shade.
But they're just a swim lane after the starter
gun's echo, a fishy twitch in the limbic lobe
almost a millennia ago. Maybe we had
a hearth, maybe a few tools.

Limbic lobes and spindle cells
buzz up the bonhomie that can
brim over in groups and with those we love,
our gestures of empathy.
Orcas have more lobes, more cells—
would they be, are they, compelled by fetishes
like our fetishes, compulsions like our compulsions?
I have one mind on land,
another in the sea.

III

Another pornographer, on trial
for obscenity, cited the popularity
of *Two Girls, One Cup* in his defense,
argued for his work to be viewed
in the lineage of Marcel Duchamp.
Readymade. Or perhaps he meant

the Duchamp one critic called
the transcendent pornographer
for the romance memorialized through body hair,
celluloid, satin, semen—
hand-sized casts of the body's caves.

At the Philadelphia Museum of Art, the viewer
must look through peepholes bored
in wooden doors to glimpse
the naked body on display in Duchamp's *Étant Donnés.*
Th doors are rustic and thick,
but the wood around the holes is slightly depressed,
softer as though fingertips approaching
had circled the viewpoint
before the tableau expands beyond
the frame of the viewer's gaze.

Or doesn't expand. Anyone could be forgiven
for expecting the scene continues
beyond the aperture's limitations.
The setting, the body have been crafted
with such economy
that nothing has been wasted,
nothing is where the rest of the body would be
if you could open the door,
push aside the crumbling brick wall,
and see yourself from a different perspective.

The figure behind the door
has the foreshortened limbs of an amputee,
no lower appendages or right arm.
At the vanishing point,
the bare fact of her sex, whose ugliness,
it seems, is not by design
but a consequence of the negotiation
between vision and embodiment.

The head exists. Unseeable but documented
in photographs, blank
mannequin's face, wig that's too late,
chasing something like an afterthought.
In the figure's left hand, a small gas light
really flickers, illuminating a faux-trickling waterfall,
the supersaturated landscape.
I ask the museum guard what he thought
of the body, the flickering light,
the clouds, the door—the whole thing.
It looks like a rape charge to me.
I cannot fold the distorted, headless, mutilated
bodies of Duchamp's contemporaries
into the radical openness and equality
of their manifestos and 'zines.
That night, I swim
in Meret Oppenheim's fur covered saucer,
Object (1936), stirring myself with its spoon.

IV

Hannah Wilke said *to honor Duchamp*
is to oppose him.
Hence, her playfully serious *oops*, there goes
the scarf, the jacket, the pants
in the museum's carefully calibrated air,
the photos of her knowing body,
full-figured, in the pose of the body
behind Duchamp's doors.

In Marcel Dzama's *Une Danse des Bouffons*
a life-sized Duchamp is rescued,
rebirthed through the hyperbolic sex
of his most infamous figure.
Twice it recasts as sacred and fundamental
something tired, suddenly
and surprisingly, all at once.
A joke that isn't really a joke.

The producer claims scat-fetishes are made
with what amounts to the ingredients
in an ice-cream sundae,
as if revelation of content turned
to palatable syrup the form's
sweet injury. Do the actresses know
they are in on the ha-ha?

V

In books about raising children,
the potty-training guru likes to say that to shit
is natural, to put it in a container, socialization.
She also likes to say, *the anus is a sphincter muscle,*
it opens and closes with emotion.

She tells a secondhand story of a midwife
who wants to demonstrate this notion
in terms of the cervix, also a sphincter muscle.
During her birthing class, the midwife places
a bowl filled with cash on the table.
She tells everyone that whoever
can shit in the bowl can have
the money, but no one has ever
walked out any richer.

In the parenting book I like best,
the author uses the analogy that children's selves
are likes cups that parents must know how to fill
when children are lonely, tired, hurt.
That Nerf gun? It's a love gun.
That pirate sword? It only cuts with kindness.
Lately, I've been chasing my husband and child
around the house. When I catch first one
and then the other, I show them how to crack an egg of love
over someone's head. How to use
their fingertips to spread the thick whites
and plump fresh yolks through each other's hair,
down the quivering back, all over the body.
Even the dogs want in: so we break eggs
on each of their heads, wild for their turn.

LULLABY

Overnight? No one
will sing him *Mama loves D—, oh, Mama loves D—*
to the tune of a hymn
that underpins the elastic universe
from bath to bed.

In a spasm of motherly surfeit, I baptized him
in the tub, unfaltering eye
to unfaltering eye. In children's books,
love is always a tie.

EPITHALAMIUM

Worrying that by feeding a want
I'd created
a need, by three a.m.
I'd been awake for an hour.

Where was my happy medium?
A pillow hot between
my thighs. My husband's body
the sea at my door,
sounding unto itself.

A drunk woman's voice
careened off the pavement. I waited
for the muted tone
that always follows,
something is due, is due.

The crying grew strange, stranger.
A fracas, two cats
thrashed. Thick body blows
and caterwaul.

Came a more piteous cry
directly beneath my sash.
I opened the blinds.
The feral black cat, fed by the neighbors,
held my eye, tiny once-king
of the Danes.

Did he want me to slip on
my shoes, unlock the back door,
and open the gate?
To move the large toy truck
I've used to block a gap
in the fence my dog always bays through?

I didn't go out because I couldn't see
an uncompromised endpoint.
Because then I would have entered
the taxonomy of the catfight.

Become the gangly Cat, who, wakened,
emerges to unlatch gates,
clap nude paws,
and move playthings from Established Paths
Through Dangerous Territory.

In the morning, I told my husband
when we build some kind
of intermediary structure—
portico, screened-in porch,
a three-seasons room—
I'd let that cat in.

The dogs only get more neurotic, he said.
Think of the hair, he said.

Then, *we could call him Howl.*

Before I closed the blinds, the cat-king
king of the ghosts let me go.
He staggered, taking a few good steps.
Before he vanished, he looked,
which thrilled me,
like someone who'd just given birth.

MOUNTAIN QUAIL ROAD

And then the thought: what if
you couldn't know more than what you felt
when you marked the fireflies' return
after the dull season's absence: carnal

as their bodies, flaring first in the dusk
and then the darkness, in some sort
of signal, moving toward each other
like those paper lanterns

filled with fire, the heart
as much as you'll ever be able to articulate,
swung forward by the body,
now swinging it, how the empiricist

is at our fingertips and the myths make us
bashful, abashed, when we feel the night
opening, ourselves shattered—shattered
then opening in the dumb show's irrepressible secret.

NOTES

"The Fourth Georgic" quotes David Ferry's 2005 translation of *The Georgics of Virgil*—beautiful, violent, "miraculous to tell."

"Box May Contain…" cribs a partial line from The National's "Racing Like a Pro."

"A Ragged Time" gets a little suddener with lines from Dickinson 695 and Leah Ollman's 2013 ARTNews review "Kathy Butterly." "Park Willows, May 2017" begins with an epigraph from Ariana Grande's song, "Love Me Harder" and nods to Louis MacNeice's "Snow," a knockout poem for a knockout world. I like to think these poems protect each other.

"The Rank of Things Indifferent" borrows its title and a line from Milton's *Areopagitica*.

"Par Avion Par Avian" quotes from *How Forests Think: Toward an Anthropology Beyond the Human* by Eduardo Kohn.

Aeon's short film *Flotsam and Jetsam* inspired "His Netherlands."

"Hunger, an Anniversary" is after J. M. Coetzee's *Life & Times of Michael K.*

"Breakfast in Fur"—in its kitchen sink, quotes from Tina Horn's "We Must Dismantle the False Dichotomy Between Porn and Erotica;" Holland Cotter's "Landscape of Eros, Through the Peephole;" and Jamie Glowacki's *Oh Crap! Potty Training: Everything Modern Parents Need to Know to Do It Once and Do It Right*. It also draws from Carl Safina's *Beyond Words: What Animals Think and Feel* and Lawrence Cohen's *Playful Parenting: An Exciting New Approach to Raising Children That Will Help You Nurture Close Connections, Solve Behavior Problems, and Encourage Confidence*, particularly the love gun and egg of love, as well as other sources about the production "Two Girls, One Cup" and scat fetishes.

I'm grateful for a UNT English Department travel grant to the Philadelphia Museum of Art that supported completion of poems in this collection along with monographs on Doris Salcedo, Hannah Wilke, Meret Oppenheim, Étant Donnés, and Marcel Duchamp.

ACKNOWLEDGEMENTS

Thanks to the editors and readers of these journals where the following poems first appeared, often in different form or with a different title:

Sporklet, "The Rank of Things Indifferent"

The Boiler, "Box May Contain a Baby Goat, a Book Lover, a Nagging Suspicion, an Act, Maybe Formaldehyde"

The Cortland Review, "Hour Before Bird Song"

Free State Review, "Skinny Dipping," "No Soliciting," "Avatars," and "State With the Prettiest Name: A Manifesto"

Birmingham Poetry Review, "Breakfast in Fur"

Aperçus "Pest Control"

Construction Literary Magazine, "A Ragged Time"

Cherry Tree, "Hunger, An Anniversary" and "After Reading Sally Mann's Memoir"

ellipsis…literature & art, "His Netherlands"

Guide to Kulchur Creative Journal, "Understudy"

Memorious, "The Fourth Georgic"

Thanks to all my teachers, formal and informal, then, now, ever, astral. Thanks to my former colleagues and students who inspired me. Thanks to Raina Joines, who found two of the best lines in the book. Thanks to Rebecca Morgan Frank for your poems and camaraderie and to Kathleen Graber and Katie Peterson for your poems and kind words. Thanks to Valerie Fowler for your art and use of the incredible cover image. Thank you to Barrett Warner for believing in these poems and pushing me to make them better in a very unpushy, hard-to-describe but always clarifying way, and to everyone at *Free State Review*/Galileo Press. Thanks to my parents Pam and Bob and my sister Molly, and most especially to Eric and to Des. For everything. Big love.

Jessica Murray's poems have appeared in journals including
Birmingham Poetry Review, *The Boiler*, *Booth*, *Cherry Tree*, *The
Cortland Review*, *Free State Review*, and *Memorious*. A Best New
Poets and Pushcart nominee, she lives in Austin, Texas. Her
manuscript was a finalist for Black Spring Press's Bottom Drawer
Global Writing Prize 2020. Visit murrayjessica.com.

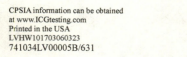
CPSIA information can be obtained
at www.ICGtesting.com
Printed in the USA
LVHW101703060323
741034LV00005B/631